Animal GIANTS!

What Kids Really Want to Know About Giant Animals

by Sara Louise Kras

NORTHWORD®
Minnetonka, Minnesota

Edited by Kristen McCurry
Designed by Lois A. Rainwater
Design concept by Michele Lanci-Altomare

Text © 2005 by Sara Louise Kras

NORTHWORD
Books for Young Readers
11571 K-Tel Drive
Minnetonka, MN 55343
www.tnkidsbooks.com

Photographs © 2005 provided by:

Digital Vision/Punchstock.com: cover (tortoise and rhino), back cover, pp. 1
(elephant), 3, 4, 5, 7, 22-23, 25, 26-27, 28-29, 30-31 (bottom), 33, 47, 50, 51, 57,
62; Image Source/Punchstock.com: cover (anaconda), p. 45;
Stockbyte/Punchstock.com: cover (bug); Creatas/Punchstock.com: pp. 1 (cobra),
41, 42; Corbis/Punchstock.com: p. 6 (top left); Sue Flood/Naturepl.com:
p. 6 (top right); Andrew Murray/Naturepl.com: pp. 6 (bottom), 49;
Corel/Fotosearch.com: pp. 8, 13; Doc White/Naturepl.com: pp. 9, 10; Photodisc/
Punchstock.com: pp. 11, 37; Stefan Klein/istockphoto.com: p. 16; Rob Stegmann/
istockphoto.com: p. 17; Jeff Rotman/Naturepl.com: pp. 19, 21, 35;
Brand X Pictures/Punchstock.com: p. 31 (top); Phillipa Lawson/Naturepl.com:
p. 34; Joe Kras: p. 36; Kevin Tate/istockphoto.com: p. 39;
Ophiophagus Hannah/Naturepl.com: p. 40; François Savigny/Naturepl.com: pp.
43-44; Doug Perrine/Naturepl.com: p. 46; P. Morris/ARDEA LONDON: p. 48;
Ben Osborne/Naturepl.com: p. 53 (top); Richard Du Toit/Naturepl.com: p. 53
(bottom left); Bengt Lundberg/Naturepl.com: p. 53 (bottom right);
Bruce Davidson/Naturepl.com: p. 54; Rod Williams/Naturepl.com: p. 55.

Illustrations © 2005 provided by:

The Granger Collection NY, NY: p. 15; Susanne Swibold/Amiq Institute:
p. 58 (top); Fine Rare Prints: p. 58 (bottom); Mary Jo Scibetta: pp. 59, 60.

Library of Congress Cataloging-in-Publication Data

Kras, Sara Louise.
Animal giants! : what kids really want to know about giant animals / by Sara
Louise Kras.
p. cm. -- (Kids' faqs)
Includes bibliographical references.
ISBN 1-55971-923-0 (hardcover) -- ISBN 1-55971-924-9 (pbk.)
1. Animals--Miscellanea--Juvenile literature. 2. Body size--Juvenile
literature. I. Title. II. Series.
QL49.K734 2005
590--dc22
2004031118

Printed in Singapore
10 9 8 7 6 5 4 3 2 1

Acknowledgments

Thanks to Tracy Marashlian's Form 4 class at Delphi Los Angeles for their assistance in creating this book; and to Russell Smith, Reptile Curator, Los Angeles Zoo; Dr. George Matsumoto, Senior Education and Research Specialist, Monterey Bay Aquarium Research Institute; and Cindy Cameron, Program Supervisor, Department of Education, San Francisco Zoo.

Dedication

To a wonderful teacher and writer, Sonia Levitin

—S. L. K.

contents

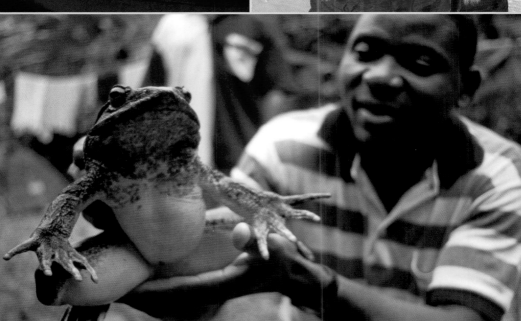

Giant animals can be found
all over the world—in the ocean, in the cold
Arctic, and in the hot rain forests.

introduction

WHAT WOULD YOU DO IF YOU WERE A GIANT?
Eat as much as you wanted? Boss others around?
These might be some of the benefits of being extra
large, but it can also be pretty hard to be a giant.
Sometimes giant animals are misunderstood. They're
not meaner than other animals, just bigger. They're
out looking for a meal just like anybody else. Of
course, being big and powerful helps them to hunt,
but they have to eat a lot more food to fill their huge
bodies than small animals do. That's a lot of work!

And what about their massive size? Giant
animals have to use more energy and muscles to move.
Just think of all the gravity weighing these giants down.
Can you imagine adding 500 more pounds (227 kg) to
your body? How about 16,000 more pounds (7,264
kg)? It would really slow you down.

One thing is for sure: giants get attention.
For centuries, scientists and kids alike have been
fascinated by big creatures and have asked some
pretty big questions. Like how did they get so big?
How many teeth do they have? How big is their
poop? And the biggest question of all—can they eat
people? Read on to find out!

What is the biggest animal of all?

The blue whale wins the prize for the biggest animal of all. At 80 feet (24.4 m) long, it's as long as two school buses. It weighs up to 150 tons (136 metric tons). The blue whale's waterspout shoots 20 feet (6.1 m) in the air, as high as a two-story building, and its blowhole is large enough to hold a small child. Powering this gigantic mammal is a heart as big as a car!

The blue whale is also the loudest animal in the world. Its call can travel 2,000 miles (3,218 km). But most of the sounds it uses are so low humans can't hear them.

Blue whales come to the surface every few minutes to blow out water and suck in air.

Blue whales are part of the baleen family of whales that appeared 15 million years ago. Their closest relative today is the hippopotamus.

How much does a blue whale eat?

This gigantic mammal feeds on miniature shrimp-like creatures called krill, and it can swallow thousands at once. Its enormous mouth has no teeth but is lined with baleen plates made of keratin, just like your fingernails. The plates look like combs made of fine hairs.

Water pours inside the whale's open mouth, expanding the whale's throat. Once its throat is full, the whale closes its mouth and pushes the water out through the baleen plates. The food is trapped by the baleen, and is then swallowed by the whale's tongue. A blue whale can eat about 40 million krill in one day!

What's the biggest fish in the world?

A shark called the whale shark weighs in as the largest fish. Despite its confusing name, it's not a whale at all. The whale shark isn't a mammal, as all whales are. It's a shark, and belongs to the fish family. The whale shark can grow to almost 65 feet (19.8 m), about as long as a large truck, and can weigh over 20 tons (18 metric tons). Its 6-foot-(1.8-m-) wide mouth is lined with small teeth that form a filter for its food. This shark may look ferocious, but only plankton and small fish need to fear being eaten by it.

How big is a sperm whale?

The sperm whale is the largest toothed whale in the ocean, growing up to 59 feet (18 m) long and weighing up to 45 tons (41 metric tons). The sperm whale also has the largest brain in the world, weighing in at 20 pounds (9.1 kg). Toothed whales are thought to be some of the most intelligent animals in the world.

Why is it called a sperm whale?

The sperm whale got its name from the spermaceti organ located in its enormous head. This organ is filled with spermaceti, which is a liquid wax. Scientists think the purpose of this organ is to help the sperm whale quickly sink to the bottom or rise to the surface of the water and float. This is important because sperm whales can dive to depths of more than 1 mile (1.6 km), and they can remain underwater for over an hour.

What does the sperm whale eat?

This giant whale dines on squid of all sizes but mainly eats smaller squid, up to 3 feet (.9 m) long. During their deep dives, sperm whales sometimes find giant squid. These squid are about as long as the sperm whale and do not go down without a fight. Many sperm whales come away with round sucker scars across their noses after battles with giant squid.

Sperm whales show off by breaching above the surface and then slapping their tail hard as they submerge.

ANIMALS

How big is a giant squid?

The largest giant squid ever found was 65 feet (19.8 m) long and weighed 880 pounds (400 kg). The giant squid is the largest mollusk, which is an animal with a soft, boneless body. It has eight thick arms 10 to 15 feet (3.1 to 4.6 m) long and two tentacles 30 to 50 feet (9.2 to 15.3 m) long, which are covered with huge suckers. The squid uses its suckers to grip its prey. With its beaklike mouth, the giant squid bites its prey and then injects venom to stun it.

The giant squid's eyeballs are truly giant—they are larger than any other animal's. At 15 inches (38 cm) across, they are as big as basketballs! These huge eyes help the squid see where there is very little light, deep in the ocean.

Can a giant squid kill a person?

It's unlikely, but it has happened. As early as the 16th century, there were reports from sailors about horrible, long-limbed beasts attacking ships. In World War II, several men were hanging onto the sides of a raft after their ship had been sunk. Suddenly, a large tentacle wrapped around one of the men and he was pulled down into the water, never to be seen again. Later, the giant squid attacked again and wrapped its tentacle around another man's leg. The man kicked and twisted his body, and eventually the squid released him.

There are recent reports of attacks, too. In 2003, off the west coast of Morocco, a yacht was grabbed, shaken, and pulled by a giant squid. The sailors stopped the boat and the squid let go. The sailors breathed a sigh of relief.

Even though there are stories of encounters with giant squids, none have ever been caught alive.

How many teeth does a great white shark have?

Another ocean giant is the great white shark. It has razor-sharp teeth, and it uses them to bite into anything that looks edible. Unfortunately, great whites are mistaken sometimes. They bite

into things such as boat motors and knock out several of their teeth. However, losing teeth is not really a problem because great white sharks are constantly growing new ones. Twenty-six teeth line the top of the mouth, and 24 line the bottom. New teeth lie flat behind these rows and move forward as replacements when a tooth is lost. One shark may go through almost 30,000 teeth during its life.

Great whites do not chew their food. They rip it into mouth-size pieces and swallow it whole.

What do great white sharks eat?

Their ideal meal would be seals, sea lions, or other sharks, which are rich in fat. Great whites have a habit of doing "taste tests" before eating a meal, taking one bite and then coming back later to finish. One scientist's theory is that the shark first bites its prey to see if it has attacked something nutritious. If the shark discovers that the fat content is too low, it will look for something else to eat instead. This could be why when humans are attacked, they are sometimes bitten only once. Humans' relatively low fat content might not be worth the shark's time.

Another scientist's theory has to do with the fact that seals and sea lions have long, sharp claws. Rather than risk getting clawed trying to eat one, the great white will take one bite to injure the animal and then return once the prey is very weak or dead.

A great white uses scent, motion, sound, and electric fields to find prey.

Do great white sharks eat their own babies?

The mother doesn't, but the first instinct of a baby shark is to eat whatever it sees. Before leaving their mother's womb, baby great white sharks, or pups, are each in a soft egg casing. Inside the womb, the pup pushes out of its egg casing and starts to gobble down its brothers and sisters as they struggle out of their own eggs.

What is an arctic lion's mane?

It is a huge jellyfish. (But they're sometimes called sea boogers—no kidding!)

Jellyfish do not belong in the fish family at all. Nor are they made of jelly. The arctic lion's mane belongs to the *cnidaria* family. This group is made up of jellies, corals, and other stinging creatures. The name arctic lion's mane comes from the animal's striking, trailing tentacles that look like a lion's mane.

The arctic lion's mane is a giant among the jellyfish. Its body can reach lengths of 6 feet (1.8 m) across with tentacles trailing over 150 feet (45.8 m), as tall as a 12-story building! The sting from an arctic lion's mane is extremely painful but rarely deadly.

This sea creature lives on the ocean surface down to about 65 feet (19.8 m). It feeds on small sea animals called zooplankton, small fish, and other smaller jellies. Because all it can do is slowly pulsate through the water, the arctic lion's mane depends on the ocean currents to move it long distances.

An arctic lion's mane moves slowly by sucking or pushing water in and out of its body through its huge bell shape.

MALS

What is the biggest animal on land?

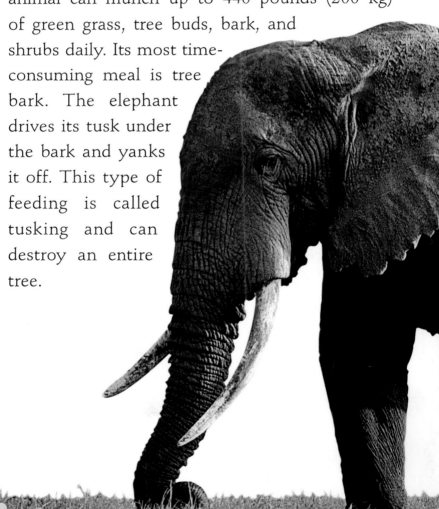

The African elephant is the biggest by a landslide. It grows up to 11 feet (3.4 m) tall and can weigh over 16,000 pounds (7,264 kg). This huge animal can munch up to 440 pounds (200 kg) of green grass, tree buds, bark, and shrubs daily. Its most time-consuming meal is tree bark. The elephant drives its tusk under the bark and yanks it off. This type of feeding is called tusking and can destroy an entire tree.

How big is an African elephant's poop?

Because an elephant has such a huge body, it makes sense that it would also have huge poop. Depending on the elephant and what it ate that day, its poop can be as large as volleyballs. Because an elephant only digests 50 percent of what it eats, its poop still has lots of food left in it, and it is gobbled up by other animals such as birds and dung beetles.

Elephants use their large tusks to gather food and to defend themselves.

Do big ears mean the African elephant can hear well?

In addition to doing important jobs like swatting flies and fanning to keep the elephants cool, their big ears do help them hear well. But these giants also use another body part to hear— they listen with their feet!

Communication is very important to elephants. They use different types of sounds. They use sounds people can hear, such as trumpeting, and other sounds that are too low for humans to hear. By spreading their enormous earflaps forward, the listening elephants tune in like a radio to hear calls from as far as 5 miles (8 km) away. Using their feet, the listening elephants can feel the ground vibrations of low calls from about 10 miles (16 km) away.

Elephants use their feet to send messages as well as receive them. If an elephant stomps its feet in fear, the waves can be felt through the ground by other elephants 20 miles (32 km) away.

The human foot is also extremely sensitive to pressures. It is thought that maybe thousands of years ago, humans used their feet to hear, too. Stand very still and listen. Can you hear with your feet?

Elephant herds communicate with each other through rumbling calls.

What's the biggest rhinoceros?

The white rhino is the biggest in the rhinoceros family, standing more than 6 feet (1.8 m) tall and weighing almost 5,000 pounds (2,270 kg).

But the white rhino isn't white at all. It's gray. (But dirt can give them a brownish hue.) Its name comes from a word in Afrikaans, a Dutch language in South Africa. In Afrikaans, the rhino was named "widjt" or "weit," both meaning wide because of the rhino's wide, flat mouth. But to the English population, the name sounded like "white" instead of "wide," and the name stuck.

A female rhinoceros and her calf have a very close relationship and will stay together for 2 to 4 years.

Is the white rhinoceros endangered?

It is listed as an endangered species because for many years white rhinoceroses have been killed for their horns. In ancient times the horns

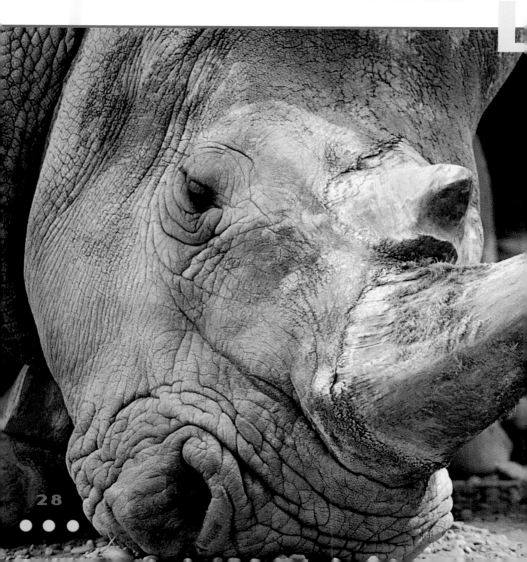

were rumored to contain magic. Some Chinese doctors still use crushed rhino horn for medicine to treat high fevers. Also, in some Arab countries, carved rhino horn is used to make very expensive knives or daggers. Because of these demands, the white rhinos were almost wiped out. Today, laws protect white rhinos from illegal hunters.

ND MAMMALS

The white rhinoceros lives on the grasslands and savannahs in northeastern and southern Africa.

Could a hippopotamus eat a kid?

Hippos may look cute, but they are dangerous. In Africa more people are killed by hippos than any other animal. Their tusks grow to 27 inches (.69 m) long and are incredibly powerful. Hippos have been known to bite a canoe or a human in two pieces. These massive creatures can be 11 feet (3.4 m) long, as tall as 5 feet (1.5 m), and weigh over 7,000 pounds (3,178 kg).

Hippos will attack in the water or on land if they're irritated. On land, a hippo can run faster than a person. If a human comes between a mother hippo and her baby, or accidentally bumps into a hippo with a canoe, the hippo will most likely attack.

Hippos do not attack people or animals to eat them. They are vegetarians who spend their evenings eating more than 100 pounds (45 kg) of grass. Their lips are perfect for all this grazing—they measure almost 2 feet (.6 m) wide. Hippos spend their days resting and staying cool in the water, which is how they got their name. Hippopotamus is Greek for "river horse."

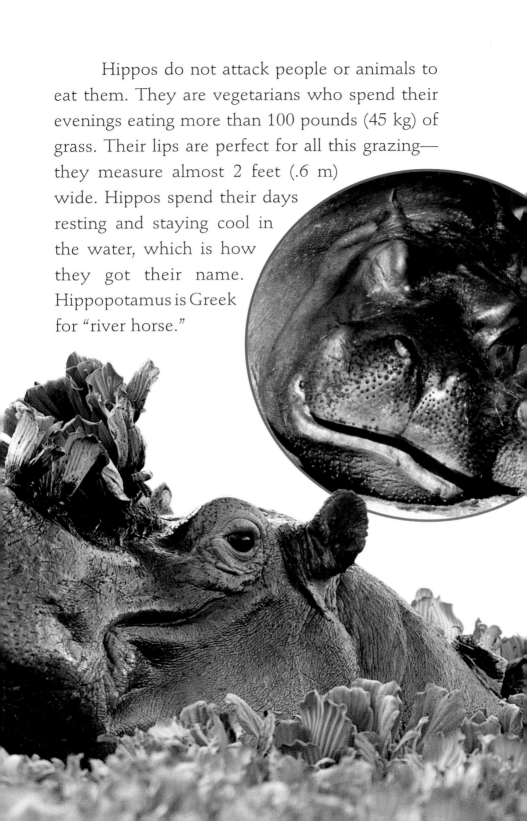

What is the biggest bear?

The polar bear beats out the grizzly and all other bears, size-wise. This 8.5-foot-(2.6-m-) long bear can weigh more than 2,000 pounds (908 kg) and lives in the icy Arctic. Polar bears are sometimes called sea bears for good reason. Their front paws are partially webbed, which makes them good swimmers. They can swim for several hours over long distances. One bear was tracked swimming 62 miles (100 km) without taking a break!

Why are polar bears white?

A polar bear looks white, but its fur is actually transparent, or see-through. Each strand of hair is really a hollow tube that absorbs sunlight, and the sun's reflection makes it appear white. The tube passes the heat from the sun to the bear's black skin underneath. This skin and a 4-inch (10-cm) layer of blubber help keep the polar bear warm.

LAND

A polar bear can smell food through 3 feet (.9 m) of snow.

MAMMALS

What is the biggest reptile in the world?

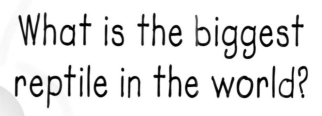

The Australian saltwater crocodile tops out at 2,200 pounds (999 kg), about the weight of a Volkswagen Beetle car. It can reach lengths of more than 20 feet (6.1 m). To keep up its enormous figure, it eats other crocodiles, pigs, and wallabies, a small kangaroo-type animal.

When the sun rises, crocodiles bask in the sun until they are warmed up.

Crocs may drown their prey by pulling them into the water and rolling over and over—called the death roll.

Does the saltwater crocodile live in the ocean?

Saltwater crocs usually live in brackish water, or part salt and part fresh water, but they have also been seen swimming in the ocean. One was spotted 150 miles (241 km) from shore in the middle of the sea.

What's the biggest lizard?

T he Komodo dragon is the world's largest lizard at more than 10 feet (3.1 m) long and 366 pounds (166 kg). This giant lizard lives on Indonesian islands in the Indian Ocean. Some scientists

Komodo dragons are usually alone except when they get together to breed or occasionally to share a meal.

believe that the Komodo's island home may have something to do with its large size. The theory suggests that on an island, there are fewer animals competing. Over a long period of time, some animal species may grow very large if they have a plentiful food source and few predators.

What does the Komodo dragon eat?

A Komodo dragon is known for its huge appetite. It can eat 80 percent of its body weight in one meal. So a 300-pound (136-kg) Komodo could eat 240 pounds (109 kg) of meat at a time!

A Komodo uses its sense of smell to look for prey. It swings its head from side to side, whipping its long, yellow, forked tongue in and out to taste the air. Inside the Komodo's mouth, the two tongue tips touch the Jacobson's organ. This organ sends a message to the Komodo's brain that tells it the distance and location of the prey. A Komodo dragon can smell carrion, or the body of a dead animal, up to 5 miles (8 km) away. Komodo dragons are also ambush hunters. They hide near jungle trails waiting for animals to pass.

Komodo will eat pretty much everything, including wild boar, deer, and even other Komodo dragons. When Komodo devour their prey, they eat the skin, bones, and hooves. The only thing a Komodo will not eat is the feces, or the waste matter in the intestines. When Komodo get to the intestines, they pull them out and swing them in the air like a cowboy's lasso to empty out the feces. Once the waste is removed, Komodo devour the intestines, too. Because full-grown Komodo will eat baby Komodo, the babies roll in animal feces to keep the large Komodo away.

Even though a Komodo dragon is huge, its movements are swift.

What is the biggest venomous snake?

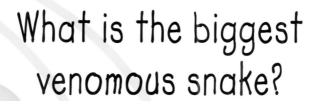

If size counts, the venomous king cobra is king of the snakes. It can kill an elephant with a single bite. Venomous means the snake contains a poison that comes out through its fangs. Humans will die within 30 minutes after a bite from a king cobra if they are not treated. The king cobra is not an aggressive snake, though. It would rather be left alone and will only attack if it's bothered.

This snake can be 18 feet (5.5 m) long, which is about three times taller than a grown man. It can rear up to a height of 4 to 5 feet (1.2 to 1.5 m), making it look as if it is standing up.

A king cobra's head is huge— as big as a grown man's hand.

Anacondas
move slower
on land than in
the water.

How big is an anaconda?

The Australian croc may be the biggest reptile overall, but when it comes to size and length combined, the anaconda wins. It can grow as long as 30 feet (9.2 m)—which is about five grown men, end-to-end—and weigh up to 1,200 pounds (545 kg). Early Spanish explorers gave the anaconda the name of *Matadora,* meaning bull killer. This name grew from exaggerated myths about the anaconda's length and body size.

Even so, the anaconda is one of the most powerful hunters in the world. Because it is a water-loving boa constrictor, it will wait close to rivers and streams, often hanging in a tree or on the ground. When other animals come for a drink, the anaconda lunges at an eye-blurring speed. It grabs the prey with its teeth, loops several gigantic coils around the struggling animal, and waits for it to suffocate. The anaconda suffocates its prey by squeezing tighter each time its prey exhales. The pressure of the anaconda's coils collapses the veins that return blood to the heart.

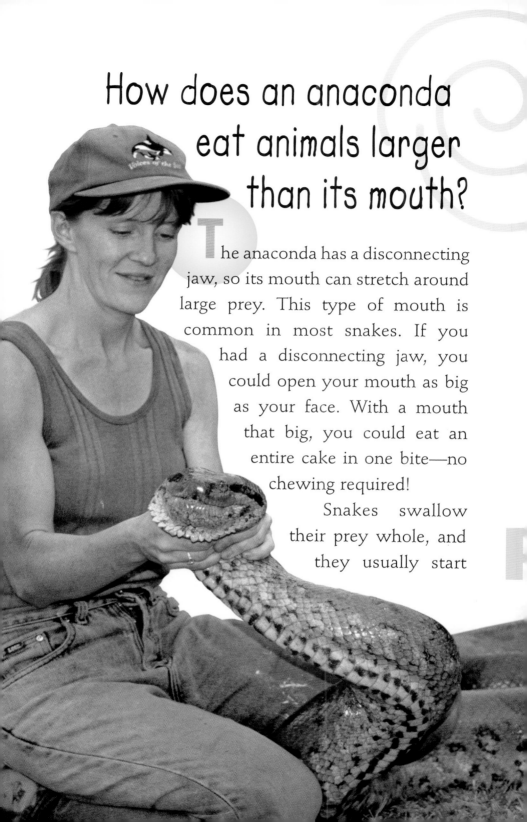

How does an anaconda eat animals larger than its mouth?

The anaconda has a disconnecting jaw, so its mouth can stretch around large prey. This type of mouth is common in most snakes. If you had a disconnecting jaw, you could open your mouth as big as your face. With a mouth that big, you could eat an entire cake in one bite—no chewing required!

Snakes swallow their prey whole, and they usually start

headfirst because the head is the smallest point. This allows the limbs of the animal to fold in, making it easier for the snake to gulp down its meal. The anaconda kills and eats storks, cranes, iguanas, deer, and fish. It has also been known to attack turtles and caiman, which are similar to alligators. One 25-foot (7.6-m) anaconda was spotted hunting, killing, and eating a 6-foot (1.8-m) caiman. After a meal like that, an anaconda may not have to eat again for weeks.

An anaconda's eyes and nostrils are on top of its head, allowing the snake to see and breathe while its body is submerged in water.

What kind of turtle is the biggest?

The leatherback turtle is biggest, and it can grow up to 8 feet (2.4 m) long, which is about as long as a large couch, and it can weigh as much as a small car—over 2,000 pounds (908 kg)!

A leatherback turtle's shell is not made of leather, but it's softer than most turtles' shells. Its shell is made out of a tissue that is tough, rubbery, and oily, and it feels like a rubber tire. The shell protects the turtle and keeps it warm when it migrates to the iceberg-filled waters of the North Atlantic Ocean.

Leatherback turtles travel farther and dive deeper than any other turtles.

Can a giant tortoise live to be 100?

Most giant tortoises can live to be 100 years old. One Galapagos giant tortoise named Harriet is thought to be the oldest living creature. In 2002, she was 172 years old. In 1835, a scientist named Charles Darwin visited the Galapagos Islands and captured Harriet when she was 5 years old.

While not quite as big as leatherbacks, giant tortoises are plenty hefty. They have been known to grow a 4-foot (1.2-m) shell and weigh up to 580 pounds (263 kg)—about as heavy as a big motorcycle.

What's the biggest amphibian?

Most salamanders are only inches long, but not the Japanese giant salamander. This giant measures 5 feet (1.5 m) long and weighs up to 55 pounds (25 kg). It lives in streams on northern Kyushu and western Honshu islands in Japan.

The Japanese giant salamander slurps down things such as fish, mice, crabs, and bugs. It pulls its prey into its mouth like a vacuum hose. Even so, it can go without eating for weeks because it digests its food very slowly.

This giant salamander was put under protection in 1951 because people were eating too many of them. Today, it is no longer part of the Japanese diet.

What's the biggest frog in the world?

Imagine a frog as big as a cat. That's the Goliath frog, and it is the biggest frog in the world. It can measure more than 1 foot (.3 m) long. It may be big, but this giant is completely silent. The Goliath has no vocal sac, so there are no giant-sized "ribbits" coming from this frog.

Goliath frogs can be found only in the wet rain forests of Cameroon and Equatorial Guinea, located in Africa. These gigantic frogs feed on insects, fish, salamanders, and smaller frogs.

Goliath frogs like to live near swift-flowing rivers in dense rain forests.

What kind of bird is the biggest?

The ostrich is an enormous bird that weighs about 350 pounds (159 kg) and can grow to 9 feet (2.7 m) tall. But this bird doesn't fly. Birds that fly have light bones. The ostrich's bones are very heavy. Because of the ostrich's weight, it would be hard for it to develop enough muscle in its wings to keep its heavy body off the ground. Even though the ostrich can't fly, it's an extremely fast runner. Its legs are thick and muscular, helping the ostrich to run along the ground at 40 miles (64 km) per hour.

This huge bird also has huge eyes. They measure 2 inches (5 cm) across and are the largest eyes of any land animal. The ostrich's long neck and sharp eyesight help it see long distances.

An ostrich does not hide its head in the sand, but it may lay its head on the ground to keep from being seen.

What is the biggest bird that can fly?

The largest flying bird is the wandering albatross. Its wingspan is a whopping 11.8 feet (3.6 m). It can be found flying over the southern oceans, often following fishing boats for many days.

In ancient times, seamen thought it was unlucky to kill an albatross. These ancient mariners thought the huge birds were the souls of seamen washed overboard, coming back to life as a bird.

The heaviest bird to fly is a tie between the Kori bustard and the great bustard. Both of these birds weigh in at 38 pounds (17.3 kg). The Kori bustard can be found in northeastern and southern Africa. These huge birds live only on land, eating small mammals, lizards, seeds, and berries.

The great bustard was once a common sight in Europe, but it was over-hunted because its meat was in great demand. By the 1830s there were no more great bustards in Britain. Today, the British Great Bustard Group is working to re-introduce these birds to England by bringing eggs from Russia and carefully monitoring the bustards as they hatch and grow. Hunting them is no longer allowed.

wandering albatross

Kori bustard

great bustard

BIRDS

How big is the biggest bug?

The Goliath beetle is a giant in both length and weight. At 4.5 inches (11.4 cm) long and weighing 3.5 ounces (99 g), this huge beetle is larger than a mouse! It can be found in western Africa. Goliath beetles feed on dead plants and animal poop, making them the housekeepers of the tropical forests.

What is the biggest spider?

The Goliath birdeater tarantula is the biggest spider around, and its descriptive name is true—this type of tarantula does occasionally snatch baby birds from their nest and eat them. These huge spiders also feast on snakes, lizards, frogs, and bats. They can be found in the coastal areas of the rain forest in South America. The Goliath birdeater spider can live for 20 years and can grow as big as a Frisbee. Now that's a big spider.

What can we do to keep giant animals from becoming extinct?

The giants of the animal kingdom are some of the most amazing animals on earth. They are part of our world's treasures. Unfortunately, almost half of the animals in this book are listed as endangered or threatened. The animals' habitats are slowly being taken away, as forests are being cut down and oceans are becoming polluted. What can we do to help out our giant friends?

We can start by sharing with people the cool things we know about giant animals and encourage them to join our effort to save them. How many people know how smart sperm whales are, or that elephants can listen with their feet? How about the fact that a mouse-sized beetle in Africa makes a pretty good housekeeper?

There are also organizations we can join, such as the World Wildlife Fund (WWF), or groups in our schools and communities that care about animals and the environment. We can organize bake sales, walk-a-thons, or even jump-rope-a-thons to raise money to donate to groups that save animals.

Changing habits at home is something else we can do. Recycling paper and plastic, and reducing how much water, electricity, and gas we use will help protect the environment and save animals' homes. So, turn off the lights, take shorter showers, and ride your bike instead of riding in a car when you can. Little things like these add up to a lot when it comes to saving giant animals.

We may feel small compared to an animal 10 times (or 100 times!) our size, but our actions make a difference. It's up to us to make sure that there's room for all animals to live on earth. Some just take up a little more space than others.

When explorers first visited the Galapagos Islands, there were 250,000 tortoises. Today there are only 15,000 left.

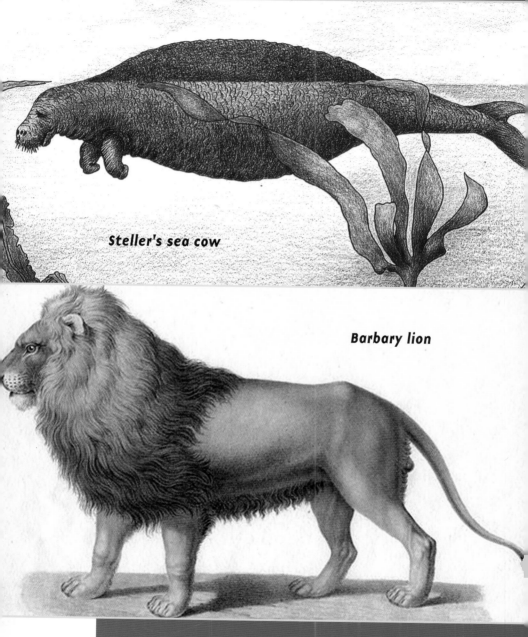

Steller's sea cow

Barbary lion

The Steller's sea cow and the Barbary lion are two giant animals that no longer swim the seas or roam the earth.

giant moa

animal giants from history

Steller's Sea Cow

Steller's sea cows were a type of manatee that lived in the arctic waters of the Bering Strait, between Alaska and Russia. The last population was discovered in 1741 when a ship became shipwrecked on an uninhabited island in this area. Despite their enormous size—25 feet (7.6 m) long and 10 tons (9 metric tons) in weight—these gentle, slow-moving creatures were easy for men to capture and kill by using a whale harpoon or large spear. Their meat was used for food and their tough hide was used to cover boats and make shoes. Twenty-seven years after they were discovered, all Steller's sea cows had been hunted to extinction.

Barbary Lion

A full-grown, male Barbary lion weighed almost 600 pounds (272 kg) and measured over 10 feet (3.1 m) from its head to the tip of its tail. The largest male lion today weighs a little more than 400 pounds (182 kg) and is 8.5 feet (2.6 m) long. The giant Barbary lion was used in gladiator contests in Rome 2,000 years ago. The last Barbary lion living in the wild was killed in 1922 in Morocco.

Giant Moa

The giant moa was a large, wingless bird that lived in New Zealand. It was almost 10 feet (3.1 m) tall and weighed about 550 pounds (250 kg), about the size of Big Bird, of Sesame Street fame. These huge birds lived in the forests of New Zealand and feasted mainly on plants. Unfortunately, giant moa were hunted to extinction by the 16th century.

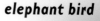

elephant bird

Elephant Bird

The elephant bird may not have looked like an elephant, but it was nearly elephant-sized at 10 feet (3.1 m) tall. It was also the heaviest bird to ever exist, weighing about 1,000 pounds (454 kg). A big bird lays big eggs, and the elephant bird's were the largest known, with a length of 13 inches (33 cm). Each egg contained a yolk of almost 2 gallons (7.6 liters)! Elephant birds lived in Madagascar and became extinct in the mid 17th century.

resources

BOOKS

CAROLINE ARNOLD. *Ostriches.* Minneapolis: Lerner Publications, 2001.

E. MELANIE WATT. *Leatherback Turtles.* Austin: Raintree Steck-Vaughn Publishers, 2001.

KARYN FOLLIS CHEATHAM. *The Crocodile.* San Diego: Lucent Books, Inc., 2001.

EULALIA GARCIA. *Giant Squid: Monsters of the Deep.* Milwaukee: Gareth Stevens Publishing, 1997.

MARIE LEVINE. *Great White Sharks.* Austin: Raintree Steck-Vaughn Publishers, 1998.

ANNE WELSBACHER. *Whale Sharks.* Minneapolis: Capstone Press, 1995.

JONATHAN GORDON. *Sperm Whales.* Stillwater: Voyageur Press, Inc., 1998.

MARY M. CERULLO. *The Truth about Great White Sharks.* San Francisco: Chronicle Books, 2000.

KATHLEEN W. DEADY. *Great White Sharks.* Mankato: Capstone Press, 2001.

SANDRA MARKLE. *Outside and Inside Giant Squid.* New York: Walker Publishing Company, 2003.

WEB SITES

http://www.amonline.net.au/factsheets/wandering_albatross.htm
Check out this site to find out about habitat, feeding, and breeding habits of the wandering albatross. You can also see a photo of the super-sized egg this bird lays.

http://nationalzoo.si.edu/animals/birds/facts/factsheets/fact-koribustard.cfm
This web site describes the Kori bustard and the conservation effort to save this land-loving bird, plus lots of information about many different animals.

http://nationalzoo.si.edu/Animals/AsiaTrail/GiantSalamanders/
The National Zoo site also has great information on Japanese giant salamanders and their Chinese cousins, including where they live and what they hunt.

http://www.extremescience.com/BiggestSpider.htm
Extreme Science provides fun facts about the Goliath birdeater tarantula and many other spiders. (Find out what kind of noise the Goliath birdeater makes!)

http://www.wcsscience.com/goliath/beetle.html
Check out this web site to see an "actual-size" picture of the Goliath beetle. (It might surprise you!)

http://www.seaworld.org/AnimalBytes/white_rhinoab.html
Sea World's web site has all the stats on the white rhino, including fun facts and conservation information.

http://www.seaworld.org/infobooks/PolarBears/pbadaptations.html
Sea World's web site also has information on polar bears, and some great photos of the bear in action!

http://www.honoluluzoo.org/komodo_dragon.htm
Click on this site to find out everything you ever wanted to know about Komodo dragons. (Did you know that this giant can climb trees?)

www.nashvillezoo.org/anaconda.htm
This web site has all the details on the anaconda and how it's different from other snakes. (For one thing, it's a lot bigger!)

http://www.sharks.com/types-of-sharks/great-white-shark.htm
This site has tons of information on this 3-ton-plus animal—including lots of great photos of the great white eating.

http://school.discovery.com/schooladventures/planetocean/bluewhale.html
Find out just how big the blue whale is at this web site. (Here's a hint: 50 people could stand on its tongue!)

http://dsc.discovery.com/convergence/giantsquid/meet/meet.html
This site takes you on an underwater expedition to find the elusive giant squid!

About the Author

SARA LOUISE KRAS has written and published more than fourteen books for kids. She has traveled all over the world and loves to write about her adventures. During her travels, Sara has seen many giant animals "up close and personal." Her favorite giant animal is the hippo.

"I will never forget one night waking up in a tent on the Masai Mara in Kenya, Africa," she says. "I heard a loud munching sound. It almost sounded like a huge machine outside the fabric walls. I pushed the canvas back and within reaching distance was an enormous hippo grazing on grass!" It's that kind of excitement that keeps her traveling.

When Ms. Kras is not traveling, she is at home with her husband, daughter, and cat, writing books for children.

photo courtesy of Joe Kras

Do you have questions about other animals? We want to hear from you! E-mail us at **kidsfaqs@tnkidsbooks.com.**
For more details, log on to **www.tnkidsbooks.com.**